"*The Bullying Workbook for Teens* is a remarkable, relevant resource for both teens and professionals. The activities are engaging and offer practical strategies to help teens work through and cope with bullying situations, while also raising their self-confidence. As I read it, I found tools to implement in my own work with teens. This book offers eye-opening insights and will be useful to any teen who has been victimized by bullies."

—Rosalind Wiseman, author of *Queen Bees & Wannabes*, the book that inspired the motion picture, *Mean Girls*

"*The Bullying Workbook for Teens* is a non-judgmental companion, reflection aid, and an 'aha' moment-maker for isolated teens. It's also a much-needed tool for clinicians. I recommend it highly and look forward to using it myself."

—Rachel Simmons, author of *Odd Girl Out*

the *i* n s t a n t h e l p
s o l u t i o n s s e r i e s

Young people today need mental health resources more than ever. That's why New Harbinger created the **Instant Help Solutions Series** especially for teens. Written by leading psychologists, these evidence-based self-help books offer practical tips and strategies for dealing with a variety of mental health issues and life challenges teens face, such as depression, anxiety, bullying, eating disorders, trauma, and self-esteem problems.

Studies have shown that young people who learn healthy coping skills early on are better able to navigate problems later in life. Engaging and easy-to-use, these books provide teens with the tools they need to thrive—at home, at school, and on into adulthood.

This series is part of the **New Harbinger Instant Help Books** imprint, founded by renowned child psychologist Lawrence Shapiro. For a complete list of books in this series, visit newharbinger.com.

the bullying workbook for teens

activities to help you deal with social aggression and cyberbullying

RAYCHELLE CASSADA LOHMANN, MS, LPC
JULIA V. TAYLOR, MA

FOREWORD BY HALEY KILPATRICK

Instant Help Books
An Imprint of New Harbinger Publications, Inc.

Distributed in Canada by Raincoast Books

Copyright © 2013 by Raychelle Cassada Lohmann and Julia V. Taylor
                Instant Help Books
                New Harbinger Publications, Inc.
                5674 Shattuck Avenue
                Oakland, CA 94609
                www.newharbinger.com

Cover design by Amy Shoup

Library of Congress Cataloging-in-Publication Data

Lohmann, Raychelle Cassada.
  The bullying workbook for teens : activities to help you deal with social aggression and cyberbullying / Raychelle Cassada Lohmann, MS, LPC, and Julia V. Taylor, MA.
    pages cm
  ISBN 978-1-60882-450-2 (pbk. : alk. paper) -- ISBN 978-1-60882-451-9 (pdf e-book) -- ISBN 978-1-60882-452-6 (epub) 1. Aggressiveness in adolescence--Juvenile literature. 2. Bullying--Prevention--Juvenile literature. 3. Cyberbullying--Prevention--Juvenile literature. I. Taylor, Julia V. II. Title.
  BF724.3.A34L64 2013
  302.34'30835--dc23
                        2012047505

Printed in the United States of America

15   14   13

10   9   8   7   6   5   4   3   2   1

First Printing

Contents

✳ contents

foreword

When I learned that Raychelle Lohmann and Julia Taylor were collaborating on a workbook to help teens better cope with bullying and cyberbullying, I was immediately so grateful and so excited.

I'm grateful because these two truly get it. As highly respected professionals in their fields, they get what it is like to be a teen in today's world, and they are committed to being part of the solution. They have clearly poured their valuable resources into this book to provide you with the tools to know how to handle being bullied, how to cope, and how to heal. Their commitment to improving the lives of middle and high school students through relevant, practical strategies has already helped thousands of school counselors, administrators, teachers, parents, and students.

I'm excited to share this workbook with the thousands of girls I work with through Girl Talk, a national organization that pairs middle school girls with high school mentors. Like me, Raychelle Lohmann and Julia Taylor are frustrated by the problem, and our frustration has led us to our passion. We are committed to developing resources that empower you to be a key part of the solution.

What I love most about this book is that it meets you precisely where you are and empowers you to take action. It is clear that the authors know that bullying is not limited to a select few or happening only in school hallways. They know it's happening through various forms of social media, and yet they get that it is sometimes what isn't said or done that hurts. They know that at some point we have all felt like we were the only ones. They also know that there are millions of young people who want to put a stop to bullying, and that is precisely why this book was written. I wish it had been available when I was a teenager! I know it would have helped me through my own experience as a victim of bullying, cyberbullying, and relational aggression.

A quote from Lily Tomlin reminds me of their efforts. "I said, *Somebody should do something about that. Then I realized, I am somebody.*" I am thankful that Raychelle Lohmann and Julia Taylor have chosen to be somebody, and I am confident that what you learn in this workbook will inspire you to be somebody, too.

—Haley Kilpatrick
Founder and executive director of Girl Talk
Author of *The Drama Years: Real Girls Talk about
Surviving Middle School —Bullies, Brands, Body Image, and More*

Dear Reader,

When you walk into class, do you automatically feel like your peers hate you because they laugh at you or whisper to one another? When you sit down in the cafeteria, do you feel lonely and undeserving of friendship? Do others refuse to look at you, speak to you, or include you in their circle of friends? If you ever feel miserable because of bullying, know that you are not alone and that there is help for you.

My name is Victoria, and I'm twenty years old. In the sixth grade, a group of girls in my class made the decision to socially isolate me. They spread mean rumors and mocked me, and they made fun of my hair and clothes. I thought their bullying would never stop. As a result of their constant harassment, I repeatedly broke out in hives. The stress often caused me to pass out, and I coughed constantly. I was diagnosed with post-traumatic stress disorder and began to have suicidal thoughts at the age of twelve. When I went to high school, things didn't get much better. Some of the same bullies from middle school were at it again, and I became the target of cyberbullying.

When I was being bullied, I felt like my life was out of control. I didn't have friends. I was hopeless and frequently sick. I thought life was not worth living. But today, life is completely different! I am happy, healthy, and free from the effects of bullying. I am a successful college student, and I travel around speaking out against bullying.

Being bullied is not a life sentence. You can move forward, make friends, and be happy. As you read *The Bullying Workbook for Teens*, you will gain the tools necessary to cope with the situation you are now in and to end the bullying. This workbook can help guide you as you seek support and take the steps to set yourself free from bullies.

Wishing you success,

Victoria DiNatale

what is bullying?

---

you need to know

Bullying is a form of abuse. It is repetitive, aggressive behavior intended to harm another person.

If you've been targeted by a bully, you've come to the right place. This workbook will help you develop the coping strategies and skills you need in order to deal with bullying. To begin, let's take a look at the types of bullying, why some people bully, and how it affects the victim.

What are the types of bullying?

- Verbal: name calling, mocking, threatening, gossiping, or spreading rumors

- Physical: hitting, punching, pushing, stealing personal property, or any other form of physical aggression

- Social: ignoring, isolating, or excluding peers from social activities

- Psychological: stalking, taunting, harassing, or intimidating

- Cyber: bullying through electronic devices; for example, texting, e-mailing, IM'ing, posting on social media, or uploading lewd or offensive pictures

Why do people bully others?

- They want to feel popular.

- They are jealous.

- They want to feel powerful.

- They feel threatened.

- They want to escape their problems.

- They feel insecure.

What are the effects of bullying?

- Emotional problems (such as stress, anger, depression, or anxiety)

- Physical problems (such as headaches, stomach cramps, vomiting, loss of appetite, or skin breakouts)

- Withdrawal from friends or social activities

- Decline in schoolwork

- Nightmares or poor sleep

for you to do

Name the types of bullying you're experiencing.

_____

_____

Write down what the bully does to you. For example, does the bully repeatedly pick on you or make fun of you for the same thing?

_____

_____

Why do you think the bully has chosen you?

_____

_____

Tell how bullying is affecting your life.

_____

_____

Tell what you want to achieve by using this workbook.

_____

_____

and more to do

Write a letter to a person who is bullying you. Let the bully know how his or her actions are affecting you. You won't actually give this letter to the bully, so you can write openly about what you're thinking and feeling.

Dear _____,

Today I, _____, am taking the first step to regain control of my life. You've singled me out and picked on me for too long. Enough is enough, and I won't take it anymore. I am going to equip myself with the tools I need to work through my feelings, build my confidence, and cope with bullying.

When you _____, I feel

(Write down the ways you're being bullied.)

anxious   angry   annoyed   ashamed   scared   sad   _____

(Circle all that apply; use the blank line to add other feelings.)

You've been doing these things since _____.

I want you to stop _____

_____.

(List the things you want the bully to stop doing to you.)

Remember when _____

_____?

(Write about one of your worst experiences with the bully.)

Well, that's not going to happen again. I am

determined   brave   confident   strong   secure   fearless   _____

(Circle all that apply; use the blank line to add other feelings.)

and I am taking the power away from you right now.

Confidently,

_____

(your signature)

you need to know

What you write in this workbook is confidential. You can explore your thoughts and feelings in private with one exception: if you think you're in danger of being physically hurt by someone or if you have thoughts of harming yourself, get help immediately. Your safety always comes first.

As you work through this book, you will be asked to explore some very sensitive and possibly uncomfortable topics. It's not uncommon to feel vulnerable when you're exposing things about yourself that bother you. Sometimes people don't feel comfortable talking about things that are troubling them, so they keep their concerns bottled up even if they're in danger of being hurt or of harming themselves. But if they told someone, they might feel better and get the help they need. By acknowledging your feelings and learning to cope with what's happening, you'll become a stronger person.

It's going to take time to see the change occur. One good way to make sure you are working toward change and are keeping yourself safe is by making an agreement with yourself because your safety comes first.

for you to do

Create a Safety First Agreement by initialing beside each statement. Use the blank lines to add your own ideas. Think of trusted adults that you can share your agreement with (for example, a parent, a teacher, or another trusted adult).

I agree that my safety comes first. I will get help immediately if

_____ I am in physical jeopardy.

_____ I feel threatened.

_____ I begin to panic.

_____ I feel like there is no hope.

_____ I begin to pull away from people and lose interest in things I once enjoyed.

_____ I have thoughts of harming myself.

_____

_____

_____

List the people you will give a copy of your agreement to.

_____

_____

_____

Keep your agreement in a place you can easily get to. Refer to it when you feel like your safety is in jeopardy.

and more to do

Copy this statement onto a sheet of paper and sign your name to it. Keep it somewhere accessible, and reread it often to remind yourself how important your safety is. Remember: Tell a trusted adult if you ever feel that your safety is in jeopardy.

My safety comes first. I promise that I will get help immediately if I ever feel like someone is going to hurt me or if I have thoughts of harming myself. No one has the right to hurt me, and if they do I will report them. I promise not to harm myself because I am needed and I am loved. I have a unique purpose in this world, and no one can fill that purpose but me.

3   ignore, respond, or tell

you need to know

There are times when you can ignore bullying, times when you should respond, and times when you should tell a trusted adult. It's important to know the difference.

Do you know what to do when you're in a bullying situation? Do you ignore the bullying? Do you take a stance and respond? Do you tell? In a tough situation, it can be hard to decide. Evaluating the bully's words and actions can help you figure out what to do.

Start by asking yourself, is the action or comment

- hurtful but not intimidating?

- a onetime offense or repetitive?

- something that can easily be ignored?

- hostile or threatening?

Next, use these guidelines to help you determine which course of action to take:

1. Ignore bullies who are just trying to get a rise out of you, if their words or actions aren't a big deal. Some situations are short-lived and die down on their own.

2. Respond to any action or comment that is not hostile or threatening. Bullies prefer easy targets, not ones who stand up to them. If you take a stance and respond, they may pull back and leave you alone, or they may test you to see whether you'll cave in. When a bully decides to test you, have a firm comeback, like "That's not true," or "Stop spreading those lies."

3. Tell a trusted adult immediately if your physical safety is being threatened. No one has the right to harm you, and any threat to do so is serious. Also, tell if someone has posted sexual material about you online. And finally, tell if you feel like you're spiraling into a black hole that you can't get out of. When you're targeted, you may feel like there's no end in sight, but that's not true. Adults can help.

for you to do

Write your own personal guidelines for determining the best course of action.

I will ignore bullying when _____

_____.

I will respond to bullying when _____

_____.

I will tell someone when _____

_____.

and more to do

Describe a situation when you were bullied and had to choose the best course of action.

_____

_____

_____

_____

_____

Did you ignore, respond, or tell someone about the bully? Describe in detail the course of action you took.

_____

_____

_____

_____

_____

_____

_____

11

4 asking for help

you need to know

If you need to ask for help in a bullying situation, it's normal to feel frightened or ashamed. Most people who told someone actually felt better after telling.

Morgan felt overwhelmed. A group of girls had started a vicious rumor about her being pregnant, and the rumor had spread like wildfire! Everyone was talking about who the father was and what Morgan would do about school.

Morgan didn't know how to convince everyone that it was a lie. She was so embarrassed that she didn't want to ask for help, but this was too big for her to handle on her own. She thought, Maybe I'll make an appointment with my school counselor. I could take a friend with me. Or I could talk to my mom. I feel a little funny about doing that, but I guess I could e-mail her.

She finally got up the courage to tell her mom. To help her remember everything she wanted to say to her mom, she decided to write it down. Next, to build up her courage, she practiced reading it in front of her bathroom mirror. I can do this, *she thought.*

"Mom, can I talk to you about something really important?" Morgan asked. Then she told her mother about the rumor.

At first her mother was shocked and wanted to know why Morgan hadn't told her earlier. Then she sat and listened to her daughter's painful story.

After Morgan was finished, she thought, Whew, that didn't go as badly as I thought it might. And I feel much better!

for you to do

Describe a bullying situation you may need help with.

_____

_____

_____

Whom will you tell? _____

How will you ask for help? _____

_____

What will you say? _____

_____

_____

Practice your script, and then ask for help.

and more to do

Describe how you felt before you asked for help. For example, were you frightened that you'd get in trouble or that asking would make things worse?

_____

_____

How did it go? _____

_____

How did you feel afterward? _____

_____

Did it play out like you thought it would? Explain what you thought would happen and what actually happened.

_____

_____

_____

_____

_____

taking steps against cyberbullying 5

you need to know

Cyberbullying is bullying that occurs through the use of computers, cell phones, and other electronic devices. Because technology allows bullies to harass others anonymously, victims of cyberbullying may not even know who is responsible. If you are being cyberbullied, there are many steps you can take to get help.

Cyberbullying can take different forms:

- Threatening someone by e-mail, IM, or text messages, or on social media sites

- Revealing someone's secrets online to embarrass or humiliate that person

- Gossiping or saying mean things online while pretending to be someone else

- Using a website to make fun of somebody else

- Taking inappropriate photos of someone and posting them online without that person's permission

Maria's story suggests some of the steps you can take.

Maria was concerned that someone had been posing as her online. She had received threatening messages from another girl that said that Maria had better stop making nasty comments about her, but she had not actually made any of those comments.

Maria knew that she shouldn't respond to any of the threats directly, so she told her father what was going on. He asked whether she had given out her password. Maria remembered giving a friend one she used a few months ago, so she logged on to all the sites where she used that password and changed it.

Next, Maria and her father printed out both the messages that were threatening and the ones that she had supposedly written; that way, even if the girl deleted her messages, Maria would still have a record of them. Then Maria deleted the comments that had been posted from her account. She took all the messages to her school the following day so she could show them to the principal. Her principal contacted the school resource officer who handled cyberbullying, and she investigated the situation.

It wasn't easy for Maria to tell her father what was going on, and she was really nervous about taking the documents to school. However she knew it was the right thing to do and wanted the bullying to stop.

for you to do

Describe a time when you were cyberbullied. Reread the steps Maria took, and decide what you could have done to prevent the online attack or to stop it from escalating. Use the space below to write your thoughts.

_____

_____

_____

_____

_____

_____

_____

_____

and more to do

Take a stand against cyberbullying. There are many different websites, advocacy groups, and organizations that help prevent cyberbullying. See whether your school or community has a club or organization you can get involved with. If not, why not start your own? Advocacy can help raise your self-esteem and empower others to make a difference.

cyberbullying or not? 6

you need to know

Technology is part of our everyday lives, and most teens are constantly connected. It can be difficult to walk away from an unpleasant or stressful situation because technology allows it to follow you everywhere. But not all unpleasant or stressful situations are cyberbullying.

Online situations that hurt your feelings may be mean, wrong, and completely unnecessary, but they are not always cyberbullying. Two of the four scenarios below involve cyberbullying; others do not.

Situation 1

"This girl at school called me a slut online. She is really popular and everybody saw it. I took my account down and it got worse. Everyone said it must be true since I canceled my account. The next day it had spilled into school. Now people call me horrible names, boys make sexual remarks to me, and my friends don't want to talk to me because they are afraid everyone will make fun of them, too. This has been happening for two weeks, and I feel like I can't escape it."

Situation 2

"My friends went ice skating and didn't invite me. They posted pictures of themselves online and talked about how fun it was."

Situation 3

"This boy in math takes pictures of me. He makes me look really ugly and writes mean things on them, then posts them online. I told my teacher, and he just tells him to put his phone away, but he never does. I started skipping math and got in trouble at school. Nobody understands how much this hurts, and I don't know how to make it stop."

Situation 4

"My friend and I got into a fight and she called me oversensitive. Then she wrote online: some people are like so oversensitive—I can't deal!!!! *I know it was about me."*

for you to do

For each of the four situations, tell whether you think it represents cyberbullying or not, and explain your answer.

Situation 1

_____

_____

_____

Situation 2

_____

_____

_____

Situation 3

_____

_____

_____

Situation 4

_____

_____

_____

and more to do

If you are in a situation that you define as cyberbullying, it's important to tell an adult you trust. Cyberbullying is often ignored or not reported.

How can telling an adult help the situation? _____

_____

_____

What might keep you from telling an adult? _____

_____

_____

Make a promise to yourself that you will tell an adult if you are being cyberbullied. And even if what's happening is not cyberbullying, you still may want to talk to someone you trust. Talking truly helps.

you need to know

Whether you've had the best day or the worst day, you should always think carefully about what you share online. Nothing online is private. If you wouldn't want something posted on a highway billboard, it's not a good idea to put it online.

Stacie and Tanisha disagreed about something minor at the movies on Saturday night. Tanisha didn't think it was a big deal, so she didn't apologize. She thought that if she didn't bring it up again, Stacie would forget about it.

To Stacie, it was a big deal. She went home and posted "Tanisha is such a selfish bitch" on a social media site. Within minutes, people were commenting and asking what had happened. Four other people from school quickly reposted it, and by Sunday morning, the original post had been shared twelve times.

Tanisha was furious with Stacie for making her the subject of gossip at school. Stacie had done serious damage to their friendship.

for you to do

Read the statements below and circle "Public" or "Private" to indicate whether you think the statement is something you should share online or keep offline. Then, explain why you chose your answer.

"First home game tomorrow … this one better not be rained out."

              Public   Private

Why _____

"I've had the worst day ever and nobody cares."

              Public   Private

Why _____

"Luv my bestie. XOXO"

              Public   Private

Why _____

"Things I HATE: snow, teachers, and HER."

              Public   Private

Why _____

"happy birthday ho! :) jk love you!"

              Public   Private

Why _____

and more to do

It's important to have an outlet to express your emotions, but in this era of social media, it's easy to forget that you can express yourself privately. The next time you feel like making an unnecessary announcement online, write about it on a piece of paper instead. After you have written down all of your thoughts and feelings, rip up the piece of paper and throw it away.

8 bullying or drama?

you need to know

It's easy to dismiss bullying as drama even when it's not. It can be scary to admit · if you are being bullied, and people who don't own up to bullying often say, "Oh, it's just drama."

Bullying and drama are very different. Drama is often associated with petty behavior, misinterpretations, exaggerated feelings, rumors, gossip, and the inability to let go of something small. Bullying may involve those, but it goes further. It is a repeated, hostile behavior intended to hurt someone physically, emotionally, or both. Read the two situations below:

1. *Janelle walks into her first-period science class, and two girls in the back of the room are whispering. When they spot Janelle, they stop. All morning, Janelle worries that they were talking about her, and she tells her friends about the situation, completely embellishing it. At lunchtime, Janelle eats with a teacher. By fifth period, everyone is spreading rumors that Janelle wants to fight the two girls.*

2. *Janelle hates going to her first-period science class because two girls in the class have been harassing her since school started. They throw things at her back, call her fat, and kick her chair, and they have even knocked her books off her desk. It's November, and she can't take it anymore. She eats lunch with a teacher every day so the girls can't sit near her in the cafeteria and do the same thing.*

The first situation is drama because Janelle has created a scenario that doesn't exist. The second is bullying. It involves repeated physical and emotional abuse that requires adult intervention.

The best way to stop drama is to stay out of it, although that may be easier said than done. Most of the time, you are aware of the people in your life who cause the most drama. If you find yourself in a situation that could easily turn to drama, try to remove yourself from it. You have more power than you think.

for you to do

Describe a situation that comes to mind when you think about the term "drama."

_____

_____

_____

Describe a situation that comes to mind when you think about the term "bullying."

_____

_____

_____

How are these situations similar?

_____

_____

_____

How are they different?

_____

_____

_____

and more to do

List the people you know who cause the most drama.

_____

_____

Think of a situation you were in that involved drama. How could you have removed yourself from that scenario?

_____

_____

How could you have avoided becoming involved with the drama?

_____

_____

Sometimes drama is not your fault or is out of your control. List two people you trust who you can talk to about this situation.

_____

just hit delete 9

you need to know

It's easy to get caught up in online drama and to post things without thinking. But whatever the situation, it's never okay to be mean, and acting that way could come back to haunt you.

You may be frustrated and want to write about the bad day you've had. You may be caught up in a fight that has nothing to do with you. Or you may be tempted to "like" or respond to an online statement that was intended to bully someone.

When you get the urge to attack someone online, it's best to just step back and try to cool off.

But what if you've already written things that, in hindsight, you wish you hadn't? For example, maybe you posted a negative comment when you were upset with a teacher after you got a bad grade on a test. Or an ex-boyfriend or girlfriend started dating someone new and you wrote something derogatory about the other person. Although all online content has potential for permanence, you can still go back and delete what you can.

for you to do

List all the social media sites you have an account on.

_____

_____

_____

_____

_____

_____

Log on to each site and read your posts. For any post that is a private matter, an online attack, or simply unnecessary, take a deep breath and hit delete. If you have photos that are unnecessary, you may want to delete those too.

and more to do

Social media is fun and a great way to engage with friends, keep up with current events, and see what's going on with distant family members. But sometimes it can consume your life. Recent studies have shown that teens who spent a lot of hours on social media sites are more likely to be depressed or anxious, or to struggle with body image issues.

Do you think you can go a day without social media? What about a week? Set a reasonable goal for yourself, and give yourself a break. Afterward, write about how it felt.

_____

_____

_____

_____

_____

10 alliances

you need to know

Alliances can be extremely helpful in combating bullying. Your allies can defend you, counteract what's being said, and, most importantly, be there for you when you need them.

Watch any competition-style reality show on TV, and you'll notice that participants form alliances to win the game. An alliance is a group of people who have your back and will stand behind you in the midst of a crisis. Paige's story is an example of how an alliance can help in bullying situations.

Paige was the target of a cyberbully who harassed, humiliated, and threatened her by sending hate messages, starting rumors, and posting inappropriate pictures of her online. Tired and depressed, Paige decided to take matters into her own hands. She'd recently watched a TV show in which the contestants formed an alliance to win the game. It's time to form an alliance, Paige thought. She used the same tactics as the contestants in the show had:

1. Pick your allies.

    Paige identified the three friends she could trust most.

2. Ask them to be in your alliance.

    Paige texted her friends and asked them to come to her house.

3. Develop a plan of action.

    Once Paige and her friends were together, she told them what was happening. Her friends were upset and agreed to defend her against the bully. Paige didn't want to attack the bully because she knew that would just make the situation worse. The group decided to start posting kind and uplifting messages on Paige's site. They agreed if they heard a rumor they would try to squelch it by telling people it wasn't true.

4. Keep the lines of communication open.

   Paige agreed to communicate often with her allies. They openly talked, texted, and defended each other online and offline.

Together Paige and her allies made a great team!

for you to do

Describe how an alliance can help you in a specific bullying situation.

_____

_____

_____

Now get ready to form your own alliance.

Whom will you ask to be in your alliance? _____

_____

How will you ask them? _____

_____

What plan will you suggest? _____

_____

_____

_____

How often will you communicate? _____

_____

What other situations can you use your alliance for?

_____

_____

and more to do

Monitoring your plan is important to help you make sure that what you're doing is actually working. If your plan isn't working, you can go back to the drawing board and change it. After one week, revisit this activity and record the following information.

Describe how well your plan is working.

_____

_____

_____

_____

Write down anything you need to change about your plan. For example, do you need to add more people? Do you need to communicate more?

_____

_____

_____

_____

11 damage control

you need to know

Your reputation is the perception that others have of you, and it's important. If you find yourself in an online situation that affects your reputation, it's time for damage control.

Have you ever seen a shipping box labeled "Handle with Care"? You know there's something fragile in that box. Just like the box's contents, your reputation is fragile. There may be things said about you that hurt your reputation, but damage control can help fix it.

Your reputation is important today, and it will continue to be important as you get older. Employers, college admissions counselors, and other people can check out your online information. Negative things about you online could skew their opinion of you, which might hurt your chances of getting a part-time job or, worse yet, getting into the college of your dreams. But don't worry; if your online reputation isn't good you can do some damage control and fix it. You can begin by using these tips to help you clean it up.

- Remove all negative comments or posts.

- Block people who are unkind online.

- Report any abuse to site operators.

- If you've made a mistake, apologize. A simple "I'm sorry, I was wrong" or "Sorry that I hurt you" can go a long way.

- Don't attack others. Two wrongs don't make a right and can lead to more problems.

- If a rumor has been started, and you feel the need to respond, keep it simple. Something like "That's not true" will suffice.

- Get friends and even family involved. Let your friends know what's going on so they can take your side by posting positive things about you.

- Periodically search for your name online. This will help you keep an eye on what's out there about you.

for you to do

Using the strategies for online damage control, help these people repair their reputations.

Miranda accidentally hit "Reply All" to a message her friend had sent to a group of twenty people. Her nasty comment was intended to go only to her friend, but instead it went to all twenty people—including the person she was making fun of.

List some damage control strategies for Miranda to try.

_____

_____

_____

Max and Lucas were friends until they both started to like Emily. Lucas got jealous when Emily started to pay more attention to Max. He began to alter pictures of Max and post them. Max heard that there were derogatory pictures of him online. Since he was no longer part of Lucas's social networking group, he couldn't access the pictures, so he asked a friend who could to pull up the site. What he saw crushed him. Right there for all of Lucas's 400+ friends to see were pictures of Max's body that had clearly been photoshopped. Below each picture was a string of insulting comments.

List some damage control strategies for Max to try.

_____

_____

_____

Describe how Lucas's actions are affecting his online reputation.

_____

_____

_____

List some strategies Lucas could use to clean up his reputation.

_____

_____

_____

and more to do

Describe a situation that damaged your reputation.

_____

_____

_____

Describe how you handled it.

_____

_____

_____

What are some strategies that might have helped?

_____

_____

_____

Do an Internet search on your name. List what you found. If you found something negative, what can you do to repair the damage?

_____

_____

_____

reducing the stress of online attacks 12

---

you need to know

People can be mean for a variety of reasons. You may not have control over what people say or do, but you do have control over how you react.

It isn't simple to "unplug" from all forms of technology, and it's nearly impossible to ignore someone who is being mean to you. Sometimes it's easy to personalize a situation and blow it out of proportion in your head, seeing or creating a problem that doesn't exist. But remember, although you may have no control over what happened, you do have control over how you react. Your actions and attitudes can reduce the stress caused by online attacks.

These strategies can help:

- Don't blame yourself for someone else's poor behavior.

- Acknowledge your feelings. It's normal to feel angry, upset, frustrated, and more when you are the target of an online attack, especially if one of your friends is the attacker.

- Tell someone how you are feeling. Talking about situations that are bothering you is a helpful outlet.

- If your friends keep bringing up the situation, ask them to stop. You can politely, yet assertively, let them know that you don't want to talk about it.

- No matter how much you want to retaliate, don't. Trying to get back at someone often causes the situation to escalate.

- Limit the time you spend on sites that provoke unpleasant feelings. Better yet, don't go to these sites at all. *You* ultimately choose where you spend your time online; choose wisely.

for you to do

Following are two situations that would evoke a stress reaction for most people. Using the stress-reduction strategies above, write about how you would take control of each situation.

Your friend started dating your ex. You said it was fine, but it really wasn't, and she knows it bothers you. Besides the daily torture of seeing them together at school, she is constantly posting things about their relationship online that irritate you.

What is stress-inducing about this situation?

_____

_____

_____

If this happened to you, what could you do to control your reactions?

_____

_____

_____

Every time you and your friend disagree about something, she blocks you online. When you confront her about it, she says, "I don't know what you're talking about; it must have been a mistake." You know it wasn't a mistake.

What is stress-inducing about this situation?

_____

_____

_____

If this happened to you, what could you do to control your reactions?

_____

_____

_____

and more to do

It can be hard to talk about your feelings, but identifying what you are actually feeling and talking about it can help. Read the feelings words below, and circle the ones you've experienced. Next time you're feeling that way, try to talk about it with a friend, a family member, or trusted adult. Add your own feelings words if you wish.

Afraid	Flustered	Perplexed
Aggravated	Frustrated	Rattled
Ambivalent	Furious	Regretful
Angry	Guilty	Resentful
Anxious	Helpless	Self-conscious
Apathetic	Hopeless	Sensitive
Appalled	Impatient	Suspicious
Ashamed	Insecure	Uncomfortable
Baffled	Irritated	Uneasy
Confused	Jealous	Unsettled
Depressed	Lonely	Vulnerable
Detached	Mistrustful	Weary
Devastated	Nervous	Worried
Discouraged	Overwhelmed	_____
Embarrassed	Panicked	_____

When people panic, they don't think clearly. They let their emotions drive their actions, which can lead to big trouble. That's why it's important to have an emergency action plan ready to follow when you get into tough situations.

Marc couldn't think straight. His heart was racing, and he was having a hard time catching his breath. Seconds earlier, he had gone online only to find a conversation happening between him and his girlfriend, Nicole—only he wasn't typing it. Someone had hacked into his account and was bashing him. What am I going to do? *Marc thought. Then he remembered his emergency action plan, the one his school counselor id in his health class one day:*

These feelings trigger my panic:

Out of control, fear, stress, helplessness

When I panic, my body gives me these warning signs:

Racing heart, can't breathe, sweating

To calm down, I can:

Take deep breaths, go outside, go for a walk

I can reach out to these people:

Mom, Coach, Jake, Chloe

Here are some things others can do to help me:

Listen and don't interrupt. Remind me that it's going to be okay. Help me come up with a plan to fix the problem.

Marc took five deep, slow breaths and then called his friend, Chloe.

"What's wrong?" she asked.

After Marc explained what had happened, Chloe suggested, "change your settings and block whoever this is. Does anybody have your password? Call Nicole and let her know what's going on. You'll be fine."

As Marc listened to Chloe, he began to calm down. He was finally able to breathe again and to think more clearly. "Thanks, Chloe. You're the best!" he said.

for you to do

With an emergency action plan in place, you won't have to think about how to respond; instead you'll be ready to act. Create your own plan by answering the questions below. Next copy your plan onto a separate sheet of paper and put it in a place that is easily accessible. Use your plan to guide you in emergency situations.

These feelings and thoughts trigger my panic:

_____

_____

When I panic, my body gives me these warning signs:

_____

_____

To calm down, I can:

_____

_____

I can reach out to these people:

_____

_____

Here are some things others can do to help me:

_____

_____

and more to do

Make copies of your plan. If you have someone you trust, you can choose to share your plan with him or her. Also place copies in some spots that you can get to easily, like your binder, locker, and backpack, or near your computer.

Write down all the places where you are going to place your emergency action plan, and put a check next to each once you put it there.

☐ _____

☐ _____

☐ _____

☐ _____

☐ _____

☐ _____

journaling 14

you need to know

Keeping a personal journal is a great way to express your thoughts and feelings. It also helps you sort through things that are bothering you.

Amaris couldn't hold her feelings in anymore. She went to her school counselor for help. "I get so worried and paranoid when people talk about me. Sometimes I even find myself believing the things they say about me," Amaris said. She sighed sadly. "I just want everyone to like me."

"Sounds like a difficult situation, Amaris," her counselor said. "Have you ever written about your feelings in a journal? Journaling can help you work through what's going on in your life."

"But I'm not good at writing down how I feel," Amaris replied.

"I understand. It's hard to write down your innermost thoughts and feelings, but there are some things you can try to make it easier. You could write them in a letter that you won't actually give to anyone. Pretending to write a letter to someone may help you see your situation from a different angle—and it may not seem so worrisome. The cool thing is that there are no rules to journaling, except the ones you make up. No one's going to grade or judge your writing style. You don't have to follow any grammar rules, like you do in school. You can use a notebook or loose-leaf binder, pencil or colorful pens; you can draw pictures or write in code. Whatever you do, pick a style that fits you."

That evening Amaris was feeling stressed. Instead of worrying about it, she grabbed some paper and started to write..

Dear Self,

Can you believe the week we've had? I feel like I am running on empty because I haven't slept much this week. When I close my eyes, I replay everything over and over again in my head. I can't believe that I'm letting others tear me apart like this. I've got to get a hold of myself ...

Twenty minutes later, Amaris put down the pen and looked at the pages she had written. Wow, it feels as if a weight has been lifted off me. I didn't realize how much I was holding in, *she thought.*

for you to do

Write a letter to yourself expressing your thoughts and feelings.

Dear Self,

_____

_____

_____

_____

_____

_____

_____

_____

_____

_____

_____

_____

_____

and more to do

For the next week, keep a journal about what's going on in your life. Try to write at least three times during the week. Since you're writing down your private thoughts and feelings, keep your journal in a safe place.

15 code blue box

you need to know

Whether it's a stuffed animal, a sentimental card, a picture, or a trinket, we all have special things that bring us comfort in life. These items often have happy memories attached to them, and they help us feel good when we're around them.

Regan was feeling down because her so-called friends were picking on her and excluding her from their conversations and outings. She used to be in with them, but not anymore. They were intentionally trying to make her feel bad. She felt so lonely and isolated.

One day her sister, Hannah, told her, "What you need is a Code Blue Box."

"What's that?" Regan asked.

"It's a box of 'feel-good' things, stuff that helps you feel better when you've got a case of the blues. I'll show you mine."

One by one, Hannah held up these items:

- A Valentine's Day card from their grandmother

- A family picture

- Her favorite poem

- A piece of fabric from her baby blanket

- A picture Regan had drawn when she was five years old

- The locket their dad had given her

"Oh, I can see how this box could really help," Regan said.

"It does. When I'm down, it helps me remember all the special people in my life. Why don't we put one together for you?"

"Let's do it!" Regan said.

for you to do

Create your own Code Blue Box. Here's what you'll need:

- A box with a lid (for example, a shoe box)

- Markers or colored pencils

- Scissors

- Construction paper, wrapping paper, or fabric

- Glue

Decorate your box and gather some special items to put in it.

and more to do

List each item you placed in your Code Blue Box. Beside each item, describe the significance it has in your life.

_____

_____

_____

_____

_____

_____

_____

_____

_____

The next time you're feeling down, grab your Code Blue Box and go through it. Recall the special memories, and give yourself a pick-me-up. You can continue to add items or change them as time goes by.

special places 16

you need to know

We all need to escape reality every now and then. When we need to get away but can't, we feel trapped. A mental vacation to a special place is one way to break free and escape our everyday problems.

Brad pulled up a text and buried his head. Brad looked at the text he had just received and felt as though he wanted to cry. Another mean text, and another unknown number. Will it ever stop? **I just need to get away,** *he thought. Suddenly, his fourth-grade teacher, Ms. Miller, popped into his head.*

One day when some of the kids in his class were having a hard time settling down, Ms. Miller had said, "Let's all go on a mental vacation. Think of a place that's special to you. It could be a place your family vacations, your uncle's house, or a private spot that you retreat to. Wherever it is, it makes you feel good on the inside when you go there." She passed out construction paper and markers, and the class began to draw their special places.

Brad remembered his picture; in fact, he still had it. He reached into a drawer and took it out. In it, he was sitting on top of the mountain near his grandparents' house. He could already feel the scene pulling him ….

He closed his eyes, and he was hiking up the mountain to a big rock. The sun shone on his face, and its warmth felt good. He could hear the waterfall below, and above his head birds soared over the treetops. The air smelled of fresh pine and new foliage. It was pure freedom. Up there, the world seemed so small, and nothing else mattered.

Brad opened his eyes and took a deep breath. For the first time in a long while, he felt at peace. **I need to do that more often,** *he thought.*

for you to do

Where is your special place? Where does your mind go when you need a break? It's okay if it's a fictional place or a place you've never been to but want to visit someday. All that matters is that it's your special place and your escape from reality.

Describe your special place.

_____

_____

_____

_____

Next, get comfortable and relaxed. Take a deep breath, and let your imagination tug you from reality to your place. Pay attention to how you feel. Focus on your senses: the sounds, tastes, scenery, things you can touch, and scents.

Describe what you experienced with each of your senses.

_____

_____

_____

_____

Tell how you felt when you were in your special place.

_____

_____

_____

_____

and more to do

Make something that reminds you of your special place. Here are some ideas:

- Draw a scene.

- Paint a picture.

- Create a collage.

- Start a scrapbook.

Put your artwork somewhere easy to remember. The next time you need a break, grab your work and take a mental vacation to your special place.

17 just breathe

you need to know
Sometimes when people are bullied they become stressed and their breathing becomes shallower. When that happens, oxygen doesn't get to the brain quickly; which can make you feel more panicked. The good news is that stress can be eased with proper breathing.

The hustle and bustle of everyday life can cause you to feel stressed. In stressful times, it's important to slow down and take deep breaths. Deep breathing has many benefits. Just check out what those deep breaths can do for you:

- Increase your energy level

- Reduce your muscle tension

- Improve your blood circulation

- Improve your skin's appearance

- Help you sleep better

So the next time you feel stressed, remember to breathe deeply.

for you to do

Practice deep breathing. Here's what you'll need to do:

1. Find a comfortable place that's free from distraction.

2. Turn off anything that might make noise.

3. Sit or lie in a comfortable position.

4. Close your eyes, and imagine having a big bubble wand in your hand. Take a deep, deep breath. Now slowly release all the air from your lungs, and fill that bubble. Imagine blowing the world's biggest bubble. Repeat.

5. Watch your bubbles drift off into space.

6. Repeat this exercise until you feel completely relaxed.

and more to do

Describe how your body felt after taking really deep breaths.

_____

_____

What thoughts were you having as you watched your bubbles drift away?

_____

_____

Give this a try: Take three quick, shallow breaths. Now take three slow, deep breaths.

Describe how the shallow breaths made you feel in comparison to the deep ones.

_____

_____

Describe times in your life when this deep breathing technique could be helpful.

_____

_____

_____

you need to know

Exercise is extremely important. Not only is physical activity essential for your health, but it can also help clear your mind and improve your mood.

Did you know that just thirty minutes of physical activity a day can stimulate brain chemicals that help calm you down and relax? If you avoid exercise or have never been an athlete, you just need a physical activity that works for you and fits into your schedule.

Some activities require special equipment or an organized group, and you can check to see if there are facilities in your community. You probably won't find snow skiing in Florida, and it's not likely that there is a lot of horseback riding in the heart of New York City—but there is a form of exercise for everyone. The key is finding what suits you, what you can commit to, and what you truly enjoy so you are more likely to keep it up. If all else fails, you can always turn on your music and dance!

for you to do

Circle any activities below that you currently do or are willing to try. Use the blank lines to add other activities.

Aerobics	Hockey	Skiing
Archery	Horseback riding	Sledding
Badminton	Jogging	Soccer
Baseball	Jumping jacks	Softball
Basketball	Kayaking	Stretching
Bowling	Lacrosse	Surfing
Boxing	Martial arts	Swimming
Canoeing	Mowing lawns	Tennis
Cheerleading	Pilates	Volleyball
Cycling	Push-ups	Walking
Dancing	Racquetball	Washing cars
Diving	Raking lawns	Weight lifting
Fishing	Rock climbing	Yoga
Football	Rope jumping	Other
Frisbee	Rowing machine	_____
Gardening	Running	_____
Golf	Sit-ups	_____
Gymnastics	Skateboarding	
Hiking	Skating (roller or ice)	

Of all the activities you circled, which can you commit to on a regular basis (at least thirty minutes a day, five days a week)?

_____

What activity on the list have you always wanted to try, but haven't for one reason or another?

_____

What obstacles might you face when trying to be more physically active?

_____

Has anything or anyone ever stopped you from exercising (for example, your self-confidence, your coordination level, or your athletic ability)? Write down what happened.

_____

_____

Keep in mind, you don't have to be a star athlete to be active.

and more to do

Pick one day a week to make an activity schedule. On that day, list what you are going to do during the upcoming week, when you are going to do it, and for how long. For example:

Day	Time	Activity
Monday	4:30–5:15	Walk around the neighborhood
Tuesday	Day off	
Wednesday	5–5:30	Swim laps
Thursday	7–8	Yoga
Friday	6–6:30	Mix it up: jumping jacks, running in place, stretching
Saturday	2:00-4:00	Play basketball with friends
Sunday	Day off	

Keep a record of your activity (you can use a simple spiral notebook), and note your mood before and after exercise. Try not to be intimidated, and remember that it sometimes takes a while to find what you truly enjoy.

you need to know

Being bullied, being treated poorly, or fighting with a friend can take a real toll on your confidence. In these situations, it's easy to forget the important qualities you have. But, like everyone else, you have strengths and characteristics that make you unique.

Stupid! Ugly! Worthless! *were the names that James repeated to himself. He had heard these words time and time again at school and online. It seemed as if no one liked him, and he was beginning not to like himself either. His confidence was shrinking, and he knew he was doing more harm than good by constantly focusing on the negative. Yet he couldn't stop checking what others were posting about him online.*

His brother, Kyle, walked into his room one night when he was online. James had his head in his hands and was crying.

"What's up?" Kyle asked.

James lifted his head and quickly brushed away his tears. "Nothing."

Kyle walked over and looked at the screen. "Oh, man, is that crap still going on? Why do you get on there all the time when all it's doing is tearing you apart? Have some confidence in yourself. Think about what you're good at and what makes you stand apart from others."

James smiled. "You sound like Mom, Kyle," he said, but he knew his brother was right.

for you to do

Respond to the questions that follow by writing down all the amazing things about yourself. You probably have more great qualities than you even realize! When you are finished, bookmark this page and add to it when you're feeling down. If you need more space, you can use a separate sheet of paper.

What would your family say are the five best things about you?

1. _____

2. _____

3. _____

4. _____

5. _____

What is your strongest character trait? _____

If you asked your friends to describe you, what is the top thing they would say?

_____

Write about a time you did something kind for a friend.

_____

_____

Write about a time you made a mistake and overcame it.

_____

_____

What are you really, really good at?

_____

and more to do

Create your own personal inspiration center. You can use a corkboard with pushpins or a piece of poster board and tape. Cut out words, images, or quotes that inspire you, and gather awards, fun photos, or nice notes that others have written to you. Arrange them any way you'd like, and add to them often.

20 clever comebacks

you need to know

Clever comebacks are witty responses that can leave bullies speechless because they weren't expecting you to say anything back. They can be effective in taking a stand against bullying, but you have to know how to use them.

Here are some dos and don'ts to follow when using clever comebacks:

Do

- Take time to think before you react to a bully, especially online. You don't want to give the bully any ammunition to use against you.

- If you're face-to-face, keep your expression neutral so that your feelings are not revealed. If you're online, try to stay as cool as possible in your responses, rather than showing how the bully's words are affecting you.

- Appear confident.

- Stand up for yourself both online and in person. It's okay to say things such as "Stop" or "That's not true."

Don't

- Respond out of emotion. Lashing out in anger can actually backfire on you, both online and in person.

- Insert insults into the conversation.

- Raise your voice. If you're online, don't use all caps when you type; this is like shouting and can be taken the wrong way.

- Make threats or call the bully names, either online or in person.

- Physically attack the bully.

- Use a comeback if someone is threatening your physical safety. Physical threats should be reported immediately.

Here are some examples of how to use clever comebacks both online and in person:

Insult: UR such a moron.

Comeback: Ha ha. 2 funny. Time 2 grow up.

Insult: You're so stupid your IQ doesn't even register.

Comeback: Unless you want to compare GPAs, I'd recommend minding your own business.

Insult: UR so ugly put a bag over ur face.

Comeback: Really? That's the best u got?

Insult: You've got no friends.

Comeback: Mature, real mature. I am finished with this conversation.

for you to do

Write down at least five hurtful things someone has said to you. For each, write a clever comeback.

1. _____   1. _____

2. _____   2. _____

3. _____   3. _____

4. _____   4. _____

5. _____   5. _____

After writing down your comebacks, practice them in front of a mirror and say them like you mean them. If you like, find an adult or friend to practice them with. Practicing ahead of time will help you feel more confident and ready to respond if you need to.

and more to do

Brainstorm some clever comebacks ahead of time. That way you'll have them ready to use when you need them. Create a clever comeback to each of the following put-downs.

Text: i h8 yr guts.

Comeback: _____

_____

Face-to-face: Stupid snitch!

Comeback: _____

_____

Face-to-face: Crybaby!

Comeback: _____

_____

Text: UR a piece of crap.

Comeback: _____

_____

Post: You need to get a life loser!

Comeback: _____

_____

21 humor

you need to know

Humor can help you deal with the stress that results from being bullied. When you are in a difficult situation, you can choose to look at things negatively, or you can try to find the humor in what is happening.

It's amazing how looking for the humor in life can make you feel better! Laughing something off can

- decrease stress
- improve your mood
- increase your confidence
- improve your health
- improve friendships

Being in a slump can

- increase stress
- increase your chances of getting sick
- make you doubt yourself
- keep you from wanting to do things you usually enjoy
- keep you fixated on what's bothering you
- keep you from spending time with others

Look at how Shannon used humor to help her:

Imani was jealous of Shannon for being a better singer. In chorus, she'd do things to irk Shannon. One day she pulled Shannon's chair out from behind her, so Shannon fell when she went to sit down. The whole class erupted in laughter, and Shannon's pride was hurt. To make matters worse, Imani filmed the incident on her phone and posted it online.

The last thing Shannon wanted was to give Imani the satisfaction of knowing that she'd embarrassed her. So Shannon logged on to her site and posted:

"The funniest thing happened! I accidentally missed the chair and fell on my butt—in front of everybody!!! But don't worry if you missed it. Thanks to Imani it was all caught on tape. GR8 footage Imani! LOL."

The next day at school, people came up to Shannon and laughed with her about the incident.

for you to do

Read Cole's story below and write two different endings.

Cole was eating ice cream when a group of guys came up from behind and one of them pushed his face into his ice cream. As he lifted his head, he heard someone yell, "Say cheese!" One of the guys snapped a picture on his phone. Minutes later, the photo had made its way online and had been shared over forty times.

Finish the story in a way that shows Cole letting his negative thoughts take over.

_____

_____

_____

Finish the story in a way that shows Cole using humor.

_____

_____

_____

Which reaction will help Cole more, and why?

_____

_____

_____

Now share a time when you used humor to cope with a situation.

1. Describe the situation.

_____

_____

_____

2. Describe how you used humor.

_____

_____

_____

3. Tell how using humor affected your feelings about the situation.

_____

_____

_____

and more to do

Humorous things happen all the time, but often we don't notice them. For the next week, pay special attention to the funny things that happen around you, whether on TV, in real life, or online. Mark this page so you can record all the things you notice.

Day	Situation	What Was Funny
1		
2		
3		
4		
5		
6		
7		

Did you notice more humorous things than you normally do? Explain.

_____

_____

_____

---

you need to know

Wouldn't it be cool if you had a remote control that could make a bully stop saying or doing hurtful things? Unfortunately, you can't control what others say and do. However, you can control your own actions, and sometimes your response is enough to stop a bully in his or her tracks.

Caleb was tired of being the brunt of jokes. He was harassed not only in the hallways of school but also online. Texts from unknown numbers, anonymous posts, bashing on various sites; would it ever end?

Feeling worthless and like his life was going down the drain, Caleb finally told his baseball coach what was going on. The coach listened, then offered Caleb a few words of advice: "Caleb, most often we have no control over people or events around us, but we do have control over how we react to them. So instead of wishing things would change, ask yourself these two questions: What do I have control over in this situation? What can I do to make it better?"

Next, Caleb's coach gave him an idea: "Could you get your friends to post some positive things about you online? Maybe if the bully sees you have the support of others, he'll back off."

"Great idea!" Caleb exclaimed, as he grabbed his things and ran out the door. As soon as Caleb got home, he asked his friends to help him. As more people started to defend Caleb, the bully started to back down. Hey, this is cool, Caleb thought.

Caleb had learned a lesson: while there's a lot that you don't have control over in life, there's a lot that you do.

for you to do

For each of these situations, circle whether or not you have control.

Control **No Control**   Someone posts something mean about you.

Control **No Control**   You lash out against someone and post mean things about that person.

Control **No Control**   A group of people starts to exclude you when they hang out.

Control **No Control**   You create a website to get people to stop bullying.

Control **No Control**   Someone uploads a vulgar picture of you.

Control **No Control**   You begin to stand up for yourself.

Control **No Control**   Someone hacked into your email.

Control **No Control**   You give out your online password.

Control **No Control**   Someone takes your private information and uses it against you.

Control **No Control**   You post a picture of someone online without that person's consent.

Do you notice a pattern? Every situation that begins with "You" is within your control because you are in control. You probably also noticed that some of those situations aren't positive, like posting a picture without the person's consent. In life, you'll be faced with many negative situations. The key is to understand what you have control over and avoid the consequences associated with making a poor decision. And when you realize that you control your own actions, you can make sure those actions are good ones.

and more to do

List some things in life that you have no control over, but wish you did.

_____

_____

_____

Explain how not having control of these situations makes you feel.

_____

_____

_____

Imagine letting go of your wish to control these things and focusing instead on what you do have control over. Explain how it feels to release your need to control things you can't control.

_____

_____

_____

Describe how knowing what you do and don't have control over can help in life.

_____

_____

_____

23 accepting yourself

you need to know

Sometimes, bullies target your differences—the unique qualities you have that make you who you are. Bullies may make fun of your race, size, sexual orientation, looks, or socioeconomic class. They may try to make you feel like less of a person because of these traits. You're not. They may make you feel as if you have to change or try to be someone you're not. You don't.

Madison has a head of curly hair that is sometimes untamable. On days when it is really humid, she always wears it in a ponytail because her curls expand. A particular group of girls constantly make racist remarks about it when it's in a ponytail or ask to touch it. When that happens, Madison reminds herself that her hair is just like her mom's and that she is proud of it.

Jonathan loves fashion design and is an exceptional artist. He aspires to go to college and be a runway designer. The kids in his social studies class make fun of the way he talks and always laugh when he asks the teacher a question. They tease him about his sketchbook. When that happens, Jonathan tells himself what a creative person he is.

Like many teenagers, Krista has acne. She no longer wants to be on her soccer team because the girls always make fun of her. They say things like "Don't touch her. It's catching!" She is always excluded and has no friends or allies on her team. When she feels that way, she thinks about her older sister, who used to break out a lot but now has perfectly clear skin.

for you to do

Has anyone ever made you feel bad about yourself because of your appearance, behavior, or something else about you? Write about what happened.

_____

_____

_____

List some ways that you can be more accepting of who you are.

_____

_____

_____

Have you ever made fun of others because of how they look? If you have, explain why. How did it make you feel afterward?

_____

_____

_____

and more to do

Think about all the qualities you have that are unique to you. For example, can you play the piano? Are you on the honor roll at school? Can you bake exceptionally well? Do you look exactly like a family member you admire? Make a list, the longer the better, of your unique traits that nobody else has and that make you the incredible person you are.

you need to know

It's easy to exaggerate a situation and fall into a pattern of faulty thinking. This behavior isn't uncommon, particularly if you're accustomed to being a bully's target. However, the reality is that some things actually are just all in your head.

Kelly had recently started to hang out with a new group of girls. One day when they were leaving school, one of the girls said, "See you later," and the others all nodded. But Kelly didn't know about any plans for getting together. She was worried that her new friends were mad at her, and all evening she wondered what they were doing. She was so upset that she was unable to eat dinner or do her homework. All she could think about was why they had left her out.

The next day, she gave her new group of friends the cold shoulder and sat alone during lunch. Finally, one of the girls approached and asked whether she was okay. Kelly burst into tears and walked away.

Later that day, Kelly confided in another friend, who told the girls why she had acted so strangely. One of Kelly's new friends rushed over to explain that Kelly was not really being excluded; it was just that all the other girls played volleyball and that the previous evening was their team party.

for you to do

Complete the following statements.

A time I thought the worst of a situation was _____

_____

Thinking the worst affected me physically by _____.

Thinking the worst affected me socially by _____.

Thinking the worst affected me emotionally by _____.

Thinking the worst affected my family by _____.

Thinking the worst affected my friends by _____.

In reality, this is what happened: _____

_____

This is what I'll do differently the next time I get caught up in faulty thinking:

_____

Worrying never accomplishes much. The next time you find yourself in a faulty thinking pattern, take a deep breath and confront your worries. You may find that your "problem" isn't really a problem at all. It's all about how you see it.

and more to do

Talk to a close friend or someone in your family about faulty thinking. Ask the person you choose to describe a time when he or she experienced faulty thinking.

Describe the situation.

_____

_____

What did this person think the outcome would be?

_____

_____

What was the actual outcome?

_____

_____

What did you learn from this person's experience?

_____

_____

25 reframing negative thoughts

you need to know

Thoughts are constantly and automatically going through our heads. We then make assumptions and interpretations of those automatic thoughts that influence how we feel and act. Not all the assumptions and interpretations we make are true, and recognizing errors in our thinking can help us feel better and act the way we want to.

Self-bashing is when you beat yourself up and play negative messages over and over in your head. These messages might involve names others call you or how you feel about yourself. You can learn to replace negative thoughts with positive ones.

For as long as he could remember, Kurt had been told he was stupid and useless. Each time he replayed those messages in his head, Kurt felt horrible. He couldn't stand to look at himself in the mirror, so he stopped taking care of himself. He no longer cared about school or his social life. His grades started to slip, and he was pushing his friends away.

One day his science teacher, Mr. Long, asked him to stay after class. "Kurt, I'm really worried about you," Mr. Long said. "You haven't seemed yourself lately. Is something wrong?"

After some tactful questioning, Mr. Long finally got Kurt to share his feelings. By the end of the conversation, Kurt was near tears as he said, "I'm a loser. A stupid, worthless loser."

Mr. Long responded, "Kurt, you've got to stop bashing yourself. You're a great young man who has a successful life ahead of him. In fact, you're one of my most promising students, but you're sabotaging yourself with all this negative self-talk.

"I think I may have something that will help. It's a tool my school counselor taught me when I used to bash myself. It's called reframing and it's simple to do. You take a negative thought and change it to a more realistic and positive one. Like 'No one cares about me.' Well, we know that's untrue. If I didn't care, I wouldn't be here now. What about your parents? Your sister? Your friends? See, there are a lot of people who do care about you. So when you have that self-bashing thought, replace it with: 'That's not true. Mr. Long, Mom,

Dad, Sis, and my friends Jake and Lance do care about me.' Now it's your turn. What if I called you stupid?"

Kurt thought for a moment, then said, "Stupid? I don't think so. I just got the highest grade in the class on your test!"

"You've got it, Kurt!" said Mr. Long.

For the first time in ages, Kurt smiled as he left class.

for you to do

Take the self-bashing statements below and reframe them into more realistic, positive ones.

I'm a loser.

_____

I can't do anything right.

_____

I'm stupid.

_____

I hate myself.

_____

I'm too fat.

_____

Everyone makes fun of me.

_____

I am so ugly.

_____

No one loves me.

_____

Now add your own self-bashing statement and then reframe it.

_____

_____

and more to do

For the next week, record each time you bash yourself. Write down what you thought and then reframe it.

Date	Situation	Self-Bashing Thought	Reframed Thought

How did you feel when you self-bashed?

_____

_____

How did you feel when you reframed your negative thoughts to more realistic, positive ones?

_____

_____

26 the isolation trap

you need to know

Everyone likes to feel good, but that doesn't happen all the time. When you're being bullied, it's easy to fall into a trap and become isolated. Sometimes the only way to get out of the trap is to force yourself to do the very things you enjoy, but have been avoiding.

Savannah's self-esteem had plummeted because a group of girls at school were making fun of her. She wanted to be accepted and fit in, but that wasn't happening. Lately, Savannah had started to spend too much time in her room, not returning calls or texts from her friends. She had even stopped going to basketball practice, something she loved.

One day her mother asked, "Savannah, what's wrong? It's as if you've shut yourself off from the real world."

"Ever since Alexis and her group stopped hanging with me, I've been in a slump, Mom. I just want to stay in my room."

"Life can't stop because you're upset and aren't being treated kindly. Sounds like you're caught in an isolation trap. You're not hanging out with your true friends, and you're letting people who don't like you affect your relationships with those who do. Not to mention, you haven't been to basketball practice in three days. The coach even called to check on you."

Savannah sighed. "I don't like living like this, but I don't know what to do."

"For starters, you've got to get up and move. You have to break free by forcing yourself to do something you enjoy, even if you don't feel like doing it. Like basketball; you love it, but because you don't feel good about yourself, you're avoiding it. Don't let someone else keep you from doing the things that make you happy. Okay, enough Mom advice. What do you say we go shoot some hoops?"

Reluctantly, Savannah got up and went outside with her mom. After fifteen minutes of shooting hoops, she began to feel somewhat better. Practice tomorrow, she thought. I'm going to do it!

for you to do

Write about a time when you were caught in an isolation trap.

How long were you in the trap? If you're still in it, how long have you been there?

_____

What things did you avoid doing because of the trap?

_____

_____

How did you break free from the trap? If you're still trapped, how can you escape it?

_____

_____

_____

If you're having difficulty identifying what you can do to break free, start by making a list of things you enjoy doing. Choose one of the activities you listed and do it.

After you've done the activity, describe how it felt.

_____

_____

_____

and more to do

It's important to do things that make you feel good, especially if you're in an isolation trap. Take time each day to do an activity you enjoy. Use the chart below to keep track of how it affects you.

Day	Activity	How I Felt Before	How I Felt After
Monday			
Tuesday			
Wednesday			
Thursday			
Friday			
Saturday			
Sunday			

self-defeating speech 27

---

you need to know

When you introduce what you are about to say with a discrediting statement, you are using self-defeating speech. In effect, you are bullying yourself. With practice, you can learn to speak with confidence.

People use self-defeating speech for different reasons. For example, beginning a sentence by saying "This may sound stupid, but…" or "I probably don't know what I'm talking about, but…" may reflect a lack of confidence.

You probably would never tell friends that what they are saying sounds ridiculous or that they have no idea what they are talking about, so why would you present yourself in that manner? Falling into a pattern of self-defeating speech can affect how other people see you. Yareli's story is an example:

Yareli is her own worst bully. She spends most of her day putting herself down both in her head and in front of others. For example, before she gives her opinion to her friends, she often says, "You probably won't agree, but…." Yareli plays lacrosse, and no matter how well she does, she always tells others how poorly she played. At school, she apologizes for asking "too many" questions, and when she needs help from a teacher, she usually starts off by saying, "This might be annoying, but…."

for you to do

Rewrite this conversation to reflect confidence, not self-defeating speech:

Student: I know I'm an idiot, but I don't understand how you got the answer to that math problem.

Teacher: I explained it twice.

Student: I'm sorry. I'll just read my notes again.

Student: _____

Teacher: _____

Student: _____

Now write about a time when you used self-defeating speech.

_____

_____

_____

What could you have said instead to reflect self-confidence?

_____

_____

_____

and more to do

Keep a journal for a week to see how often you use self-defeating speech. Each time you make a self-defeating comment, rewrite it to be positive. Try to become aware of how much you use self-defeating speech in order to lessen the behavior. Remember, if you wouldn't say it to a friend, why would you say it to yourself?

Confidence takes practice and won't happen overnight. Make a conscious effort not to say negative things about yourself. Beginning a sentence with "I know I'm probably wrong, but…" discredits whatever you're about to say. You're better than that. Give it a try.

28 depression

you need to know

Being bullied can lead to depression. Depression is a deep state of sadness. There are many different symptoms of depression, including hopelessness, feelings of rejection, poor concentration, lack of energy, sleep problems, and sometimes suicidal tendencies. If you feel like you are depressed, ask for help. It is never a good idea to keep depression a secret.

Stephanie walked into her counselor's office and burst into tears.

"What's wrong, Stephanie?" Ms. Jenkins asked.

Stephanie poured out the story of how her best friend had turned on her and gotten all their other friends to turn on her too. They were excluding Stephanie from their outings and treating her like she didn't exist. A few had even blocked her online and sent her mean messages stating that they didn't ever want to talk to her again. As though that weren't enough, they were spreading lies and rumors about her, and people believed them! This had been going on for months, but she had been afraid to ask for help.

"When I go home, I don't have anything to do so I sleep all afternoon. Then I can't sleep at night so I get online. I cry all the time, and I've lost weight. To top it off, I've slacked off at school, and now I'm afraid of failing. I just feel like it's hopeless. What's wrong with me?"

Ms. Jenkins replied, "Stephanie, it's not hopeless. It sounds like you've got some big things going on that are keeping you from enjoying your life. You were very smart to come and talk to me. I can help."

for you to do

How much do you know about depression? Take the myth or fact quiz below to test your knowledge.

Myth or Fact

1. Depression is an illness. ☐ ☐

2. A person who is sad has depression. ☐ ☐

3. You can get over depression by just thinking happy thoughts. ☐ ☐

4. Anyone can get depression. ☐ ☐

5. Anger in teens can be a symptom of depression. ☐ ☐

6. Something bad has to happen to cause depression. ☐ ☐

7. Talking about depression will make it worse. ☐ ☐

8. If left untreated, depression can result in risky behavior. ☐ ☐

9. Depressed people are loners. ☐ ☐

10. Professionals can help with depression. ☐ ☐

If you are experiencing symptoms of depression, please seek help.

Answers

1. **Fact.** Depression is an illness caused by a combination of hereditary, biological, psychological, and environmental factors.

2. **Myth.** Sadness can be a symptom of depression, but just being sad doesn't mean a person is depressed.

3. **Myth.** Depression is an illness. Happy thoughts will not make it go away. People who have depression will need treatment to overcome it.

4. **Fact.** Depression can affect people of any age, any ethnicity, and any gender—anyone.

5. **Fact.** Anger, irritability, and agitation (even over small things) are signs of teen depression.

6. **Myth.** Depression isn't always connected to bad events in life. In fact, depression can occur when everything is going great.

7. **Myth.** Everyone needs outlets to talk about their feelings, and talking can actually help with depression. Talking about an illness like diabetes doesn't make it worse. The same is true with depression.

8. **Fact.** Many teens who suffer from depression try to self-medicate by turning to alcohol, drugs, or sex to help them with their inner turmoil. Depression can cause reckless decisions and lead to academic, family, and social problems if left untreated.

9. **Myth.** Depression can affect anyone, even the most popular person at school. Isolation is one of the many symptoms of depression, but not all depressed people isolate themselves.

10. **Fact.** Professional treatment does help with depression. Treatment may include medication, therapy, or alternative approaches.

and more to do

Have you ever felt like there's no hope? Put a check next to each statement that is true of you.

- ☐ 1. I feel sad more often than not.

- ☐ 2. I don't like to hang out with my friends anymore.

- ☐ 3. I'm more jumpy when I'm around a lot of people.

- ☐ 4. I sleep a lot more than I used to.

- ☐ 5. I have a lot of trouble concentrating.

- ☐ 6. My grades have dropped.

- ☐ 7. I'm easily angered and frustrated for no obvious reason.

- ☐ 8. I've lost weight.

- ☐ 9. I've gained weight.

- ☐ 10. I am always worried about what others think of me.

- ☐ 11. I feel like people are talking about me all the time.

- ☐ 12. I feel alone.

- ☐ 13. I don't have anyone I can turn to.

- ☐ 14. I cry a lot more than I used to.

- ☐ 15. I have panic attacks.

- ☐ 16. I've stopped doing things I once enjoyed.

- ☐ 17. I get tired frequently.

- ☐ 18. Sometimes I feel like it would be better if I weren't around.

- ☐ 19. I have thoughts of harming myself.

- ☐ 20. I have tried to harm myself.

If you checked any of these statements, please speak with an adult. **If you checked 18, 19, or 20, please get help immediately.** No matter what you're dealing with, harming yourself is not the answer. There is help. Please speak with your school counselor, teacher, coach, parents, minister, or another trusted adult. If you feel like you don't have anyone to talk to, call the National Suicide Prevention Lifeline at 1-800-273-TALK (8255).

Depression will not go away on its own. There are people who care about you and want to help. Please reach out to them; you don't have to go throughout this by yourself. If you're working with a counselor or therapist, take this activity along to your next session. It can help you begin a conversation about your feelings and help the counselor better understand what's going on in your life.

you need to know

It's never good to bottle up any emotion, especially anger. When you hold in anger, you're not dealing with what's bothering you, and that can lead to negative consequences. Instead of keeping your anger bottled up, you can express it in appropriate ways.

Brent was tired of being made fun of. He tried to ignore it, but it was getting really old. If he heard the word "fag" one more time, he thought he'd explode. One day, a former friend sent a text during class to Brent: "sup fag?" That was it! When Brent saw the message, he threw his phone clear across the classroom.

Shocked, his teacher sent Brent to Mr. Michaels, the principal. Brent was so angry that he could barely talk to Mr. Michaels.

"Brent, this isn't like you," Mr. Michaels said. "You're one of the most laid-back people I know. What happened?"

Brent told Mr. Michaels about everything that had been going on and ended with "I just couldn't take it anymore."

"Have you ever heard the story of the straw that broke the camel's back?" Mr. Michaels asked. "Well, that text was it. You've been bottling this stuff up for so long, it had to come out somehow. You have to find an outlet to release that anger. What's more, you've got to deal with what the problem is and handle it immediately; don't hold it in until it eats at you. You can begin by recognizing and avoiding, if you can, the things that set you off. Then find healthy ways to release your anger and frustration. Maybe you could go for a run or work out your anger in a video game. You could try writing or painting or drawing. Whatever outlet you choose, use it."

Brent left Mr. Michaels's office feeling like a weight had been lifted from his shoulders. He saw his friend Chase in the hall and went up to him. "Hey, you up for some hoops after school? I've been stressed and really need to blow off some steam."

Brent had decided that he was going to start addressing situations head-on; no more bottling them up. He didn't want another episode like today's to ever happen again.

for you to do

Do you keep things bottled up? Explore the things that frustrate you.

List things that trigger your anger.

_____

Describe how you usually respond to anger.

_____

_____

Describe a time when you exploded.

_____

_____

What were the consequences?

_____

_____

Were there things you could have done beforehand to prevent the blowup?

_____

_____

We all need outlets to release anger; for example, gaming, writing, exercising, reading, or calling a friend. List some of your outlets.

_____

_____

and more to do

Draw the outline of a bottle. Inside, write frustrating things that you're bottling up. Beside each thing, write how long it's been bothering you: a week, a month, a year?

What can you do to release your frustration about each of these things?

_____

_____

_____

30 irrational fear

you need to know

When we are afraid of something, we sometimes let our fear consume us. We lose sight of what's really happening and let our imagination take over. This may lead to anxiety, worry, and stress. The good news is: there are things you can do to keep your fear from consuming you.

Gabby hadn't been acting like her bubbly self for a few days. After she bombed a quiz, her math teacher asked her to stay after class to chat.

"Gabby, I've noticed that you seem a little down and you're not sitting with your friends anymore. Also, you failed the quiz, and you could have aced that in your sleep, What's going on?"

"Nothing, it's no big deal." Gabby retorted.

"Well, I suspect it's something, and I'd like to help. Are you sure you don't want to talk about it?"

Gabby took a deep breath and said, "All of my friends hate me. Everyone at this school hates me because of the new girl. She thinks I hate her and I don't. I never did or said anything about her. She is making everyone turn against me."

"Wow, that's a lot to worry about. How did this start?"

"I don't even know. One day we were all hanging out, the next we weren't. I came into lunch late and there was nowhere to sit, so I had to sit with other people and nobody talked to me. Then I got mad and didn't speak the rest of the day. They all hate me."

"What makes you think they hate you? Have they said anything to you?"

"Well, not really. But they didn't even try to make room for me at lunch. Everything was great until she moved here. They like her better than me and it's like I don't exist anymore."

"Gabby, have they said anything to make you think they don't want you around them?"
"No."

"Have they told you that you can't sit with them?"
"No."

"I understand how you're feeling and I have a question for you. How much of your fear is real? You haven't tried to talk to them, you moved your seat in class, and you haven't been sitting with them at lunch. Maybe they think you're mad at them."

"I don't know. Maybe?"

"You don't know what they are thinking until you talk to them. I know this is a tough situation for you. It's important to keep irrational fear from consuming you. Let's talk about some strategies to help you cope if this happens again."

Together, Gabby and her math teacher fought fear with FEAR:

Familiarize: Write down your fears really quickly. Don't think too much about them. If something pops into your head, write it down.

Gabby's list included a fear that her friends would like the new girl better and eventually ditch her.

Evaluate: Check to see whether each fear you listed is real or perceived (one you made up).

The teacher asked Gabby a series of questions to help her see that there wasn't any evidence supporting her fear.

Actions: Look at how your fears are affecting your actions.

Gabby took a deep breath and said, "Well, I guess I am avoiding them because it's easier for me to be mad at them. I want to be in control of this, but it's just making me crazy and I cannot think about anything else."

Reality: Look at what's really happening.

"Gabby, could it be that you're afraid that the new girl has taken your place? Are you jealous and afraid she'll take your friends away from you? Don't let your imagination make this into something it may not be."

When Gabby left class she had a better understanding of what she was feeling and had a clearer picture of what was 'really' happening.

for you to do

Try the FEAR formula with your own personal bullying situation. If you need more space, use a separate sheet of paper.

Familiarize: As quickly as you can, write down your fears about this situation.

_____

_____

Evaluate: Record whether each fear you listed is real or perceived.

_____

_____

Actions: Describe how your fears are affecting your actions.

_____

_____

Reality: Write down what the real fear is.

_____

_____

List some things you can do to help you deal with the situation.

_____

_____

and more to do

Tell about a time when you let your fear distort reality.

_____

_____

_____

Describe how fear can negatively impact your perception.

_____

_____

_____

Explain how relying on just your perception can lead to trouble.

_____

_____

_____

Describe how the FEAR formula can help you separate reality from perception.

_____

_____

_____

31 anxiety

you need to know

Anxiety is a feeling of distress, apprehension, fear, or worry. Being bullied can exacerbate feelings of anxiety and even cause physical symptoms, but with the right tools you can control your anxiety.

The bell rang, and it was time for gym. Rachel had been dreading gym all day. She hurried to the locker room, hoping to be the first one in and out, but it was too late. Tameka, Brianna, and Amanda were already waiting for her.

They sneered at Rachel when she walked in. Rachel tried to avoid them, but they moved closer to her. Rachel felt the sweat bead on her forehead, and her heart pounded in her chest. I'm going to faint, she thought.

Just then she heard a commanding voice from across the room: "STOP!" It was Julie, the captain of the volleyball team. Silence followed, and Tameka, Brianna, and Amanda scurried out of the room.

"You okay?" Julie asked as she approached Rachel.

"I think so, thanks," Rachel said.

"How long have they been treating you like that?" Julie asked.

"Too long, and it's only getting worse. Sometimes I get so anxious that I think I'm going to die."

"I used to be that way. I remember freaking out over little things. I thought I had asthma because I would gasp for breath, but my doctor said it was anxiety. Luckily, I've got it under control."

"How did you do that?" Rachel asked.

"It wasn't easy, but I realized that stressing about situations wasn't helping me deal with them. I started to talk about my feelings rather than stuffing them inside me, and I stopped bashing myself. Even when I wanted to hide, I forced myself to be around other people, especially the ones who cared about me. When I felt like I couldn't breathe, I took slow, deep breaths. And I put my time and energy into things that energized me rather than depleted me, like volleyball. I made it my mission to be the best volleyball player in the state. Now I'm the captain of the team."

Rachel decided that if Julie could do it, she could too. She loved to write and was on the school newspaper staff, so she thought she'd start by asking Julie whether she could write a story about her journey to success in volleyball. Rachel was already feeling more in control and confident she could get the upper hand on her anxiety.

for you to do

Identify situations and events that cause you anxiety.

_____

_____

_____

Describe what your anxiety feels like.

_____

_____

_____

List some things you do to alleviate anxiety.

_____

_____

_____

Describe how you feel after you do these things.

_____

_____

_____

and more to do

Anxiety can be manageable. During the next week, keep a record of how your anxiety affects you, what you do to alleviate it, and how well your actions work.

Day	What Provoked My Anxiety	How My Anxiety Affected Me	What I Did to Alleviate It	How It Worked
Day 1				
Day 2				
Day 3				
Day 4				
Day 5				
Day 6				
Day 7				

Describe any patterns you noticed in the events that cause you anxiety.

_____

_____

_____

_____

How did the anxiety alleviators work? Which ones worked best?

_____

_____

_____

_____

you need to know

Being mean is never okay. However, having a clear and true perception of why someone is acting a particular way can help you understand that person's actions. Empathy is the ability to identify with another person's point of view. In order to feel empathic toward others, you first need to try to understand what they might be feeling or thinking.

Casey's father had lost his job, and her family was having a hard time financially. Casey used to be able to buy the clothes she wanted, go to the movies every weekend, and her family would often take her friends out to dinner. Now they were struggling just to pay the bills.

Casey was embarrassed and didn't want to tell anyone what was going on. Instead, she began to distance herself from her friends. Casey's friends thought she was angry with them, so they started to spread rumors about her. Over time, it turned into a dramatic ordeal and nobody knew what was really going on.

After Casey said some very mean things about her former best friend, Andrea, she finally confronted her. Casey broke down and confessed what was really going on, and she apologized for her behavior.

Casey hadn't realized how much her mean and isolating behavior was hurting Andrea. Andrea hadn't understood the reasons behind Casey's behavior. Neither had communicated properly to understand where the other was coming from. With Andrea's help, Casey was able to talk to her other friends about what was happening.

for you to do

For each of the following situations, write one word to describe how you would feel.

Your parents are going through a rough divorce, while all your
friends' parents are happily married.   _____

You just moved to a new town and don't know anyone.   _____

Your best friend gets mad at you and posts a reveals you   _____

You and your best friend have a fight, and she posts pictures of herself
with other people at the restaurant you two always hang out at.   _____

Your parents don't have enough money to buy you a new outfit for
the school dance, so you wear the one you wore to the last dance.   _____
Someone points it out to everyone.

It is easy to make judgments about others if you don't understand the situation. It's
also easy to take a situation personally if you don't know the whole story. The next
time you find yourself jumping to a conclusion, try to empathize with the other
person.

and more to do

Kindness and empathy go hand in hand. When you practice kindness, you build awareness about how others are feeling, and kindness can be a helpful expression of empathy toward others. Everyone should practice random acts of kindness on a daily basis. Hold doors open, offer assistance to those in need, or help a younger sibling who is having trouble with homework. The idea is not to make a big deal out of being kind, but to just make it a part of your daily routine.

Practice one random act of kindness a day for the next week and write what you did, how it made you feel, and how the person receiving your kindness seemed to feel.

Day	What I Did	How I Felt	How the Other Person Seemed to Feel
Day 1			
Day 2			
Day 3			
Day 4			
Day 5			
Day 6			
Day 7			

And don't stop just because the week is over: keep being kind!

33 real friendships

you need to know

A real friend makes you feel good about yourself. Real friends have trust, respect, and compassion for each other. If someone doesn't make you feel good about yourself, you might want to evaluate the friendship.

You may associate with a lot of people or have a ton of "friends" on social media sites, but how many of those are real friends? Real friends are honest, loyal, kind, helpful, and dependable. Good friends trust each other, laugh together, care about each other, don't stay mad at each other, share, give each other space, and have each other's backs. A real friendship is not one-sided; each of you acts as a friend to the other.

for you to do

Do you try to be a real friend? Do you have friends you don't treat well? Sometimes when friendships aren't going well, you have to decide whether the person is a real friend.

How do you want friends to treat you?

_____

_____

_____

How do you treat your friends?

_____

_____

_____

If you are not treating your friends the way you want to be treated, it's time to change. Write down three steps you can take to be a better friend.

1. _____

2. _____

3. _____

and more to do

List the qualities that are important to you in a friend; for example, loyalty, dependability, trustworthiness, honesty, and a sense of humor.

_____

_____

_____

_____

_____

_____

_____

_____

Now think about your friends. Which friends have some the qualities you listed? Which friends do not? For those who don't, think about what each of you brings to the friendship and whether or not it's worth keeping.

you need to know

Toxic friends don't make you feel good about yourself. They take from the friendship but seldom contribute, leaving you drained and lonely. It's best to learn what an unhealthy friendship looks like and get out of it quickly.

Authentic friendships are an important key to happiness. It isn't uncommon for people to surround themselves with people who bring them down, without understanding what is wrong with these friendships. Toxic friendships leave you exhausted and often wondering whether your friend is mad at you, is talking about you, or is going to exclude you. A toxic friend may:

- be fake

- withhold information from you

- always bring you down

- talk about you behind your back and then deny it

- talk badly about your other friends

- brag too much

- make fun of you, then say, "Just kidding"

Do these characteristics sound like the qualities of any of your friends?

for you to do

Chances are, a friend you think may be toxic probably is. Circle the responses that best describe your friendship with this person.

If I told my friend a huge secret, my friend

1. would never tell anyone.

2. might tell a few friends.

3. would tell everyone.

If I'm having a bad day, I

1. would tell my friend everything; that's what friends are for.

2. would tell my friend that I'm a little down, but not why.

3. wouldn't tell my friend anything; the whole world would find out.

If I started spending less time with my friend to spend more time with a girlfriend or boyfriend, my friend would

1. be happy for me and understand.

2. understand, but still constantly ask me to hang out.

3. try to break us up and never leave me alone.

If we had plans and a better offer came along, my friend would

1. keep our plans.

2. lie to me about everything.

3. tell me, straight up, that something else came up and exclude me.

When we make plans to hang out

1. we both decide what to do.

2. I always decide what to do.

3. my friend never lets me decide what to do.

If you circled mostly 2's and 3's, it's probably time to evaluate your friendship. All friendships hit roadblocks, but if your friend's behaviors frequently leave you feeling bad, it's time to go. Breaking up with a friend is hard to do. There is hurt on both sides. But in the long run, it's the right thing to do.

and more to do

If you're in any toxic friendships, you may need to let them go. First, you have to identify whether your friendship is toxic. Think of one or more friends, and respond to these questions.

What do you like about your friendship? _____

_____

What don't you like about the friendship? _____

_____

What does a real friend look like to you? _____

_____

What does a fake friend look like to you? _____

_____

What do you contribute to the friendship? _____

_____

What does your friend contribute to the friendship? _____

_____

Are your contributions equal? _____

For each friendship evaluate your answers and decide whether the friendship is worth keeping. Remember, you deserve to have friends who care about you and make you feel good.

you need to know

Sometimes friends grow apart. If you are no longer feeling supported, or if you feel like the friendship is toxic, one-sided, or more hurtful than helpful, it may be time to let it go. You deserve to have friends who don't cause too much stress and who bring you more happiness than pain.

If you've had a fight with a friend, you may be temporarily angry but still want to keep the friendship. You can give it time and seek support from others. But if you constantly find yourself wondering why you are friends with someone, you may need to walk away. Breaking up with a friend is difficult. It may be messy and cause a roller coaster of emotions. You may grieve the friendship for a while. That's why it's important to decide whether it's really what you want. Think about the following questions:

- Do you get nervous or anxious when you hang out with your friend?

- Do you ever lie to get out of hanging out with your friend?

- Is this friend possessive of you?

- Does your friend bring you down?

- Does your friendship ever make you unhappy?

If you answered yes to any of the questions, it may be time to let go.

for you to do

If you are considering leaving a friendship, first take a closer look at it and see whether or not it's salvageable.

When was the last time your friend called you out of the blue to ask how you are?

_____

Does your friend only talk about herself or himself, becoming or seeming to become disinterested when you talk about you?

_____

Does your friend ever ask you to hang out? _____

If something better comes up, does your friend cancel on you and not include you in the new plans?

_____

How much time do you spend with your friend? How much time do you want to spend with your friend?

_____

Has your friend ever really hurt you and not apologized? Worse, has this friend not even realized it?

_____

Is your friendship worth it? _____

and more to do

Moving on from a friendship is a big deal. Before writing someone off, it's important to consider what life will be like if you do decide to end the friendship.

What will it be like if you're in the same class in the future? What if you have to work on a group project together?

_____

_____

If you decide you want to be friends again, what might happen?

_____

_____

If your parents are friends, will it be weird if you have to see each other?

_____

_____

What will happen if ending the friendship causes a huge fight?

_____

_____

Do you have other friends you can truly trust and turn to for support? Who are they?

_____

_____

What will you do with anything that reminds you of your friendship (for example, put it in a shoebox, discard it)?

_____

_____

How will you know you made the right decision? How do you think you'll feel?

_____

_____

self-empowerment 36

---

you need to know

Self-empowerment is having the strength to do what is best for you. Self-empowerment means believing in your value, your abilities, and your accomplishments. It also means having the confidence to stand up for what is right and to feel good about your choices.

Self-empowerment often takes a lot of practice and positive self-talk. When you are the target of a bully, your self-esteem can easily plummet—even when you know that what the bully is saying about you is simply meant to put you down. Affirmations can empower you and help you rise above what you know isn't true.

An affirmation is a declaration of what you know to be true. It's a positive statement that reflects how you want to think about yourself, a situation, or a desired outcome. Affirmations should be repeated on a regular basis until you believe and demonstrate what you tell yourself.

Here are some examples of affirmations:

- I can do anything I set my mind to.
- I am smart.
- I am a great athlete.
- I am a good friend.
- I have a family that loves me.

- I am talented.
- I am energetic and fun to be around.
- I am a great cook.
- I can achieve my goals.

Regularly repeating affirmations will help you be stronger and better able to cope with the stress that being bullied can generate.

for you to do

Think of as many positive things as you can about yourself. List them, in affirmation style, below.

_____

_____

_____

_____

_____

_____

_____

_____

_____

_____

and more to do

Write each affirmation on a separate piece of paper or an index card. You may want to make multiple copies. Post them in places where you will see them every day (for example, on your bathroom mirror, in your school notebook, or in a dresser drawer). Repeat them every day.

37 mentors matter

you need to know

Teens who have mentors report higher self-esteem, higher self-awareness, and higher self-confidence. A mentor can offer a listening ear and sound advice to help you with problems related to bullying. Mentoring relationships can exist between adults and teens or teen-to-teen (many schools have peer mentoring programs).

Olivia had trouble making friends, and she was often teased at school for being alone. Her self-confidence had been squashed by bullies, and she was very intimidated around others. She didn't know her father, and her mother had to work two jobs to make ends meet.

When Olivia talked to her school counselor about her situation, he suggested she get a peer mentor. Olivia's mentor began meeting with her once a week. The two would talk, and her mentor would help Olivia with homework and with building her self-confidence.

With her mentor's encouragement, she joined the art club at school and made a few friends. Eventually, her new friends introduced Olivia to other people, so she had a group to sit with at lunch, do homework with, and hang out with on the weekends.

Talking helped Olivia a lot, but most important, she realized that many other teens felt like she did and that she wasn't alone. And although Olivia no longer felt intimidated by the bullies who used to laugh at her, she continued to check in with her mentor regularly.

for you to do

Write down the name of someone you know personally whom you look up to.

_____

Tell why you look up to that person.

_____

_____

_____

If that person has helped you in the past, tell how.

_____

_____

_____

What, if anything, would you like that person to help you with now or in the future?

_____

_____

_____

and more to do

Many communities have programs, such as Big Brothers, Big Sisters, that pair mentors with teens based on common interests. If you are looking for a mentor, you can check out programs in your area, or you can simply ask someone you know to fill the role. If you cannot find somebody, ask a teacher or school counselor to help connect you with a mentor.

List the qualities you would like to have in a mentor.

_____

_____

Whom would you like to be your mentor?

_____

_____

If you don't know, whom can you talk to about finding a mentor?

_____

_____

What would you like a mentor to help you with?

_____

_____

Use the space below to practice asking someone to be your mentor. Include why you need one and how it could help you.

_____

_____

_____

_____

_____

_____

_____

_____

_____

_____

_____

38 antibullying organizations

you need to know

If you are being bullied, you are not alone. Many people have dedicated their lives to helping those who are bullied, and there are organizations that provide support and guidance for teens.

Organizations like the three described below help prevent bullying, offer support for victims, and increase awareness about the negative effects of bullying.

The Trevor Project

The Trevor Project is a national organization providing crisis intervention and suicide prevention services to lesbian, gay, bisexual, transgender, and questioning youth. It was founded in 1998. *Trevor*, a short film set in 1981, is about a happy thirteen-year-old who has a crush on one of the most popular boys in school. When Trevor's peers find out about his crush, they mock and tease him. He becomes depressed and decides the world would be a better place without him. After a suicide attempt, Trevor resolves that he will no longer be a victim, and he learns to embrace and accept himself.

www.thetrevorproject.org

StopBullying.gov

StopBullying.gov is a federal government website that provides information from various government agencies on bullying, cyberbullying, who is at risk, and how to prevent and respond to bullying. This website offers prevention tips, help, and resources for teens. It includes blogs, videos, games, and information to help those who are victimized by bullying. There is even an action plan to inspire teens to create an antibullying campaign in their community or school.

It Gets Better Project

In response to students taking their own lives after being bullied, columnist and author Dan Savage and his partner Terry Miller created a YouTube video to inspire hope for LGBT youth facing harassment. Since the release of that video, the It Gets Better Project has become a worldwide movement. The site is a safe place where young people who are lesbian, gay, bisexual, or transgender can see how love and happiness can be a part of their future. It's also a place where straight allies can visit and support their friends and family members.

www.itgetsbetter.org

for you to do

Each of the organizations you just read about was started because someone wanted to help others. Imagine that you are going to start your own antibullying organization, and answer the questions below.

What would the name of your organization be? _____

Write down some goals for your organization. _____

_____

Explain your reasons for wanting to start your organization.

_____

_____

List the ways you would promote your organization. _____

_____

Whom would you get to sponsor you? _____

What would you put on your website? _____

_____

What are some steps you could take to get started? _____

_____

You just planned your own antibullying organization. If you feel passionate about this, talk to an adult and solicit the help of others to get things running. Who knows, your organization may just take off and help others who are in situations similar to yours.

and more to do

Now that you're almost at the end of this workbook, you might be thinking, *Now what?* We have compiled a host of noteworthy resources for teenagers, parents, educators, and counseling professionals at www.newharbinger.com/24502. We hope you'll take the time to visit the website and continue to think, learn, and grow.

39 moving forward

you need to know

Bullies have been around for a long, long time. While you may not be able to stop a bully from being a bully, you can use the skills taught in this workbook to help stop yourself from becoming a victim.

Mia was flipping through a magazine on her bed when her phone vibrated. She glanced at the screen and noticed it was her good friend Emma, asking "U OK?"

Emma was concerned because, earlier that day, Mia had had a run-in with a person who had bullied her in the past. Mia smiled about Emma's caring. She was such a good friend.

Mia thought back to a few months ago, when she had thought her life was over because of the bullying. Back then, the incident that happened today would have broken her, but not now. Now Mia was more confident, secure, and assertive than ever before. She had been working hard to overcome her feelings of fear, insecurity, and anxiety. Even though it had been a long and, at times, difficult road, Mia was proud of all she had accomplished. She had finally learned to accept that she might not be able to change people, especially bullies, but she refused to be a victim any longer. Mia replied to Emma, "Better than OK---I'm great!"

for you to do

Over the course of this workbook, you have been working on confronting and coping with bullying. This activity can help you see how far you have come.

When I began this workbook, I felt _____.

In doing the activities, I realized _____

_____

_____.

Now, if anyone tries to bully me, I know that I can _____

_____

_____.

The skills I could use more practice on are _____

_____

_____.

The most important thing I learned is _____

_____

_____.

and more to do

Congratulate yourself; you finished this workbook! By completing the activities, you've demonstrated that you are dedicated to taking a stand against bullying. You now have the tools to defend yourself, your friends, and your community.

Hopefully, along the way, you've picked up confidence, courage, and comfort, as well as the understanding that there is no one else exactly like you. Our world desperately needs everyone's unique talents and qualities. Don't let anyone, including a bully, rob you of your individualism. Stay strong. Be bold. Move forward.

Raychelle Cassada Lohmann, MS, LPC, is a national board certified counselor and a licensed professional counselor. Lohmann has worked as a school counselor at the middle school and high school levels, and has helped hundreds of teens deal with feelings of frustration and anger. Raychelle has participated in extensive research on anger and specializes in individual and group counseling for anger management. She is the author of *The Anger Workbook for Teens* and *Staying Cool...When You're Steaming Mad*.

Julia V. Taylor, MA, is author of *Perfectly You*, *G.I.R.L.S.* (Girls in Real Life Situations), and *Salvaging Sisterhood*. She speaks nationally about relational aggression, body image, media literacy, and other teen topics. Taylor has experience working in middle and high school settings as a professional school counselor.

Foreword writer **Haley Kilpatrick** is the founder and executive director of Girl Talk, a national nonprofit organization through which high school girls mentor middle school girls to help deal with the trials and triumphs of the tween and early teen years. She is also the author of *The Drama Years*. She lives in Atlanta, GA.

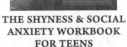